psyched for science

Super Science Projects About Sound

Allan B. Cobb

the rosen publishing group's
rosen central
new york

To my mom and dad for always encouraging my love of science and nature.

Published in 2000 by The Rosen Publishing Group, Inc.
29 East 21st Street, New York, NY 10010

First Edition

Library of Congress Cataloging-in-Publication Data

Cobb, Allan B.
     Super science projects about sound / Allan B. Cobb.
       p. cm. — (Psyched for science)
     Includes bibliographical references and index.
     Summary: Introduces the fundamentals of sound through hands-on experiments and activities.
     ISBN 0-8239-3176-5
     1. Sound—Experiments—Juvenile literature. 2. Science projects—Juvenile literature. [1. Sound—Experiments. 2. Experiments. 3. Science projects.] I. Title. II. Series.
QC225.5.C6 1999
534'.078 21—dc21
                                           99-04327
                                             CIP
                                           AC

Manufactured in the United States of America

contents

introduction

The World of Sound

Sounds are all around us. Radios, televisions, cars, planes, people, and pets all make sounds. Even the peace and quiet of the wilderness has sounds: wind rustling leaves, birds singing, and insects buzzing. Some sounds are very loud, and others are very quiet. Certain sounds, like music, can be pleasant, whereas other ones, such as a jet airplane flying overhead, are unpleasant. In this book, you will explore the world of sound.

Sound travels in waves, and sound waves have energy. You can see this energy in the vibrating strings of a guitar. The amount that the string vibrates affects the tone of the sound that is produced. Your ears carry sound waves to your brain, which interprets the waves as the sounds you hear. If you have ever thrown a rock into a pond, you heard the splash and then saw ripples move out in circles from where the rock hit the water. Sound waves are much like the ripples. They move out in all directions from the source of the sound. Sound waves continue moving outward unless something—for example, your ear—blocks them. For you to hear a sound, your ear must convert the energy in the sound waves into a vibration that your brain interprets as sound.

In order for sound to exist, there must be some material—a medium—for the sound waves to travel through. The sound we hear travels in waves through the air. It can also move through solid and liquid substances. Sound waves do not always travel at the same speed. The speed at which they travel depends on the medium that they are moving through, as well as other things. Temperature, humidity, and air pressure can all affect the speed of sound in air. One of the experiments in this book lets you actually measure the speed of sound. Then you will test how sound travels through different materials.

The experiments in this book provide detailed instructions on how to get started. Beyond that, they depend on your observations. Each activity has its own instructions and any safety warnings. Follow these carefully as you explore the world of sound.

1 Making Music with Stretched Strings

A stringed instrument such as a guitar produces sound when someone plucks or strums its strings. The vibration of the string creates a sound wave. If you have ever watched someone play the guitar, you may have noticed that the guitarist places his or her fingers on the strings to produce a single note or a chord, which is a group of notes played together. When these tones and chords are combined in an ordered fashion, the result is a series of sounds that our ears hear as music.

Each vibrating string of a guitar has a certain pitch. The pitch is the quality and position of a tone in relation to other tones. Pitch depends on the tone's frequency—the number of vibrations per second. As the pitch of a sound increases, so does its frequency. Each of the six strings on a guitar has a slightly different length. The length and tension of each string determine the exact pitch of the tone that that string will produce. Guitarists can change the pitch of the strings by pressing down on them at different points along the guitar's neck.

In this experiment, you will make your own stringed musical instrument. You will then use your instrument to explore how length and tension affect the pitch of the tone produced by a string.

- A nylon fishing line
- A 2- to 3-foot (60-90 cm) length of board, 2 inches by 4 inches
- A nail
- A hammer
- A small bucket
- Small stones or other weights
- 2 ice cream sticks

Making Music

#1 Ask an adult to help you hammer the nail into the board close to one end. The nail should be about 2 inches (5 cm) from the end of the board.

#2 Tie one end of the fishing line to the nail.

#3 Place the board on a tabletop so that the end of the board just hangs over the edge of the table.

#4 Tie the other end of the fishing line to the small bucket and hang it over the edge of the table. Don't let the bucket touch the floor.

#5 Stand the ice cream sticks on edge between the board and the string about 4 inches (10 cm) from each end of the board. It should be easy to stand the ice cream sticks on edge because of the weight of the bucket.

9

#6 Pluck the string and listen to the sound it makes.

#7 Place several small stones or weights in the bucket and pluck the string again.

#8 Add more stones and notice how the pitch changes when you pluck the string. Do this several times, adding stones each time.

Analyzing Your Results

#1 What happened to the pitch of the sound as the weight in the bucket increased? Why do you think it changed the way it did?

#2 In music, the pitch of each tone, or note, fits into a sequence called a scale. If notes are played that are not part of the scale, they are said to be off key. You may have seen someone tune a guitar by turning the peg at the head of the instrument. Look closely at the tuning mechanism. How do you think adjusting it tunes the guitar?

#3 When you watch someone play the guitar, the musician holds the neck of the instrument and touches the strings at certain locations as he or she plays. How do you think this affects the pitch of the sound produced by the guitar?

For Further Investigation

#1 Move the ice cream sticks closer together. How do you think moving them closer will affect the pitch of the sound produced?

#2 Repeat the experiment using a thicker or thinner fishing line. How do you think changing the thickness of the fishing line will affect the pitch of the sound produced?

2 Sound Cannon

Sound waves move by compressing and then expanding the medium through which they are traveling. You have already seen that the energy in the waves can cause an object to vibrate. The waves press on the medium as they vibrate outward. As they move inward again, the medium expands into the space that the vibrating wave has left. Sound waves produce a series of these compressions and expansions, which travel away from the vibrating object.

Just like ocean waves, sound waves carry energy and can exert force on objects. You may have seen a **cheerleader use a megaphone** to make her voice sound louder. The megaphone takes the sound waves from the cheer and points them in one direction. Because the waves are now directional, they sound loud to those who are in front of the megaphone. The megaphone can also be used as a funnel to collect sound and make it louder when coming from a distant source, or amplify it. You may have seen old movies or illustrations that show a hearing-impaired person using a device called an ear trumpet as a hearing aid. Ear trumpets direct and amplify sound in the same way that a megaphone does.

In this experiment, you will construct a sound cannon that uses a funnel to concentrate sound wave energy so that you can see it work. Controlling the direction and volume of sound energy is part of the branch of science known as acoustics.

What You Need

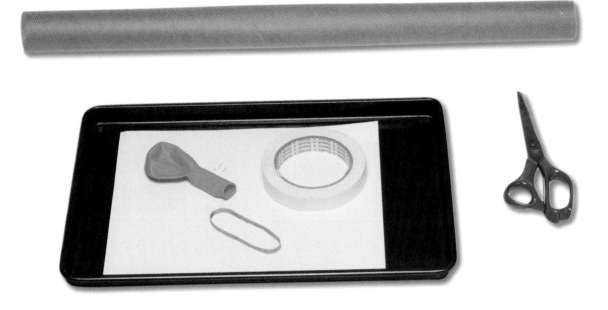

- A cardboard mailing tube, poster tube, or wrapping-paper tube
- A balloon
- Scissors
- A large rubber band
- Paper
- Tape
- A saucepan or shallow baking dish

Sound Cannon

What You'll Do

#1 Make sure that both ends of the mailing tube are open.

#2 Cut the neck off of the balloon with the scissors. Stretch the balloon over one end of the mailing tube. Make sure that the balloon is stretched tight over the end of the tube.

Secure the balloon with the rubber band.

#3 Make a cone out of the paper, and tape the side. The bottom of the cone should have a diameter of 1/4 inch to 1/2 inch (0.5 to 1 cm). Tape the cone securely onto the open end of the mailing tube.

#4 Fill the pan with water and hold the point of the sound cannon close to the water.

#5 Snap your fingers close to the end of the sound cannon and observe what happens to the surface of the water. Repeat this action with other sounds such as a radio, a friend talk-ing, or a toy that makes noise.

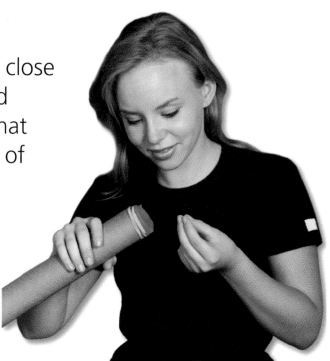

Analyzing Your Results

#1 Why do you think the cone was added to the end of the mailing tube?

#2 Where do you think the energy to move the water came from?

#3 How do you think the ripples in the pan of water are related to the sound waves?

Sound Cannon

#4 How do the ripples differ for loud sounds and quiet ones?

For Further Investigation

#1 Your sound cannon produces enough force to blow out a candle. Have an adult help you light a candle that is securely mounted in a candlestick holder. Hold the cone end of your sound cannon close to but not in the candle flame. Tap the balloon at the other end of the sound cannon and observe the candle flame. What happens? Why?

#2 Try this experiment with tubes and cones of different sizes. How do these changes affect the results?

3 Seeing Sound

Sound moves through a medium as a series of waves. The sound waves are a series of compressions and expansions. The area where the expansions take place is called the rarefaction. If you compare sound waves to the ones in the ocean, the ocean wave's crest—its highest point—is like a sound wave's compression, and its trough, or lowest point, is like the sound wave's rarefaction.

A loudspeaker works because of this same principle of compression and expansion. The speaker's cone vibrates back and forth in response to electrical impulses. As the cone moves forward, the air around it is compressed. When the cone moves backward, the air expands. The compressed and expanded air travels until it reaches your eardrum. There the energy in the sound waves is transmitted to your brain, which hears the sounds.

Our hearing process begins when sound waves strike our eardrums. The eardrum is a tightly stretched membrane (a thin piece of human tissue). When sound waves reach the eardrum, the compressions and expansions cause the eardrum to vibrate. These vibrations produce waves in the fluid inside the inner ear. This movement in turn reaches specialized cells in the inner ear called hair cells, which are attached to nerve fibers. The movement of the hair cells produces nerve impulses that the brain interprets as sound.

Sounds with different pitches or volumes produce different vibrations. In this experiment, you will explore how various sounds cause a thin, tightly stretched membrane—somewhat like your eardrum— to vibrate in different ways. You will also learn how sound waves are converted to motion in a thin membrane.

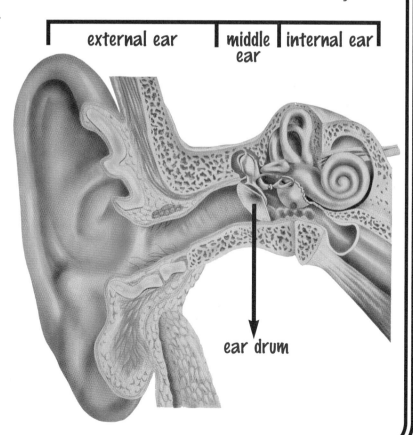

external ear | middle ear | internal ear

ear drum

What You Need

- A coffee can
- A can opener
- Scissors
- A balloon
- A large rubber band
- A small mirror
- Glue
- A flashlight

Seeing Sound

What You'll Do

#1 Ask an adult to help you remove both ends of the coffee can with a can opener. The ends will be sharp, so handle them carefully.

#2 Cut the neck off of the balloon with the scissors. Stretch the balloon over one end of the coffee can. Make sure that it is stretched tight over the end of the can. Secure the balloon with the rubber band.

#3 Glue the mirror to the stretched balloon.

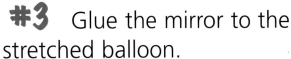

#4 After the glue has dried, lay the sound detector on its side on a table in a darkened room.

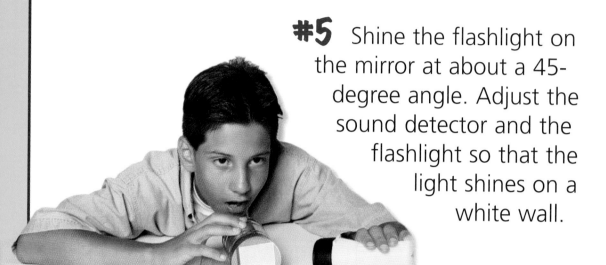

#5 Shine the flashlight on the mirror at about a 45-degree angle. Adjust the sound detector and the flashlight so that the light shines on a white wall.

#6 Yell into the open end of the coffee can and observe what happens to the beam.

#7 Try to determine the softest sound that will give a response on your sound detector.

Analyzing Your Results

#1 Which made the beam of light move more, loud or soft sounds? Why?

Seeing Sound

#2 One possible explanation of how your sound detector works is that your breath causes the balloon to vibrate. How can you test to see whether your sound detector is responding to sound or to breath?

#3 What do you think causes the balloon of the sound detector to move?

#4 How do you think the sensitivity of your sound detector would change if you used a smaller mirror?

For Further Investigation

#1 Use a flashlight with a very narrow-focusing beam or a laser pointer to make a small dot of light on the wall. Place a sheet of paper on the wall and mark the location of the beam. Make noises of different levels and mark each point where the beam shines. If you use a laser pointer, make sure that you use it only under adult supervision and be careful not to look directly into the beam of the laser.

4 Speed of Sound

The speed of sound changes depending on the medium that the sound waves are traveling through. Measuring the speed of sound in air also depends on many other factors, such as air temperature, humidity, time of day, and air pressure. As temperature increases, for example, so does the speed of sound. Measuring the speed of sound has so many variables associated with it that not all scientists agree on an exact number for its speed.

Physical obstacles affect the speed of sound waves. In canyons with steep walls, for instance, the walls affect the speed of sound waves. When sound waves in one medium (the air) reach another medium (the canyon walls), some of the sound passes into the new medium, but the rest reflects off the surface of the target medium back to the source. We hear this sound twice: once when it reaches our ears from the original source, and once when the sound waves that have reflected off the surface of the

Grand Canyon

medium reach our ears. The second sound is an echo. You can use an echo to measure the speed of sound. In this activity, you will find the speed by listening for an echo off a wall, measuring the distance, and then calculating the speed of sound.

Experiment #4

What You Need

- 2 wooden blocks or sticks
- A yardstick, a meterstick, or measuring tape
- A calculator

What You'll Do

#1 Find a large brick wall in a quiet place. The back of a building will work best.

#2 Stand and face the wall at a distance of about 30 feet (10 m). Slowly walking backward, bang the sticks together and listen for an echo. When you hear an echo, stop and mark your position.

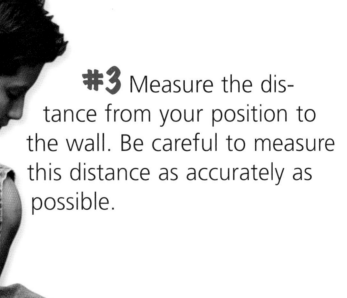

#3 Measure the distance from your position to the wall. Be careful to measure this distance as accurately as possible.

Analyzing Your Results

#1   The minimum time interval between the original sound and an echo in which the human ear will hear the echo is 0.1 second. If the echo occurs less than 0.1 second after the original sound is heard, we will not hear the echo. Thus, your echo interval is 0.1 second. Calculate the speed of sound using the following formula:

Speed of sound = distance ÷ 0.1 second
Remember to double the distance you measured because sound traveled from the sticks to the wall and back for you to hear an echo.

#2 The speed of sound in air at room temperature is 1126 feet per second (343 m per second). How does your calculated speed of sound compare to these values? Why do you think there is a difference?

#3 Why do you think it would be likely that you would hear an echo in a canyon or cave?

Speed of Sound

For Further Investigation

#1 Repeat this activity with a partner. Instead of moving backward until you hear an echo, choose a location and have a partner time the interval between the bang and the echo. Make sure that your partner stands next to you. Measure the distance as before but substitute the new time interval and distance into the speed-of-sound formula.

#2 Repeat this activity at different times of day.
Choose a time in the early morning when the temperature is cool and a time in the afternoon when the temperature is warm. If possible, record the humidity at that time from the weather forecast. You may want to repeat this activity during different seasons, such as winter and summer, for maximum temperature extremes, or with walls of different heights.

5 Sound in Solids

You have already measured the speed of sound in air and found that the speed varies under different conditions. The speed also varies according to the material through which the sound waves travel. For example, sound travels faster in water than in air, and it travels even faster in steel. If a sound travels one mile in five seconds in air, the same sound underwater would cover a mile in about one second. However, it requires only one-third of a second for sound to travel through one mile of steel.

When sound waves move through a medium, individual molecules in that medium vibrate as the sound passes through them to the next molecule. The reason that sound travels faster through liquids and solids than gases is that the molecules in liquids and solids are packed more closely together than those in gases. Solids have the most densely packed molecules of any form of matter. Because the molecules are close together, sound waves are conducted through solids quickly and efficiently.

Although sound moves faster through solids than either liquids or gases, not all solids conduct sound at the same rate. In this activity, you will explore how different materials conduct sound.

Sound Molecules in Gas

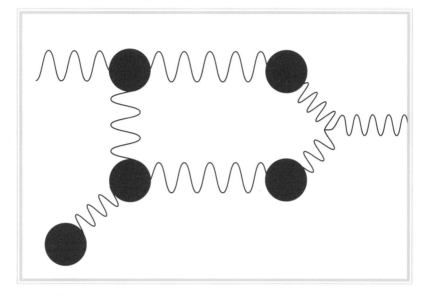

Sound Molecules in Solid

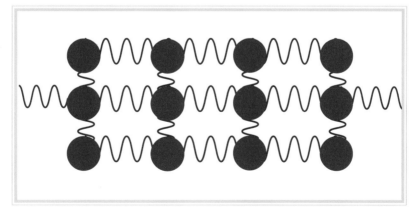

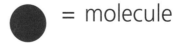 = sound wave   ● = molecule

What You Need

- A metal coat hanger
- String
- Thin wire
- Thread
- A nylon fishing line

What You'll Do

#1 Make a data table to record your observations. You can photocopy the table on the next page or make one of your own.

Sound in Solids

Material	Observations	
	First sound	Fingers in jar
String		
Thin wire		
Thread		
Nylon fishing line		

#1 Tie a 3-foot (1 m) length of string to the center of the coat hanger as shown in the diagram.

#2 Hold each end of the string with the index fingers of each of your hands. Wrap the ends of the string around your index fingers several times.

#3 Gently bump the coat hanger against a table or other hard, solid object.

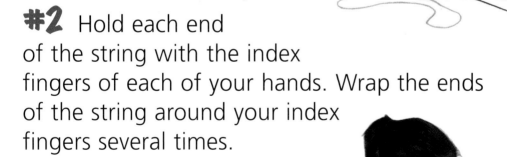

#4 Listen to the sound that is produced. Record your observations in the data table.

#5 Put your index fingers against, but not in, your ears and have a friend gently bump the coat hanger against the table again. Record your observations in the data table.

#6 Repeat steps 1 through 5 for the thin wire, the thread, and the nylon fishing line.

Analyzing Your Results

#1 Describe the first sound that you heard.

#2 How did the sounds differ when you placed your fingers near your ears? Why do you think they were different?

#3 Based on your observations, which type of material conducts sound the best?

#4 You can make a telephone by punching a hole in the bottoms of two cans and connecting them with string. As long as the string is pulled tight, one person can speak into one can while another person listens and hears what is said. Can you think of a better substitute for string in this simple phone?

For Further Investigation

#1 Repeat the experiment using pieces of string, wire, thread, and fishing line of different lengths. How does the length of material affect the resulting sound?

#2 Test the effects of cold on the transmission of sound by using the wire setup and placing it in the freezer for an hour before testing.

6 Sound in a Jar

Sound waves move by compression and expansion. The speed at which sound waves move forward depends on how close together the molecules in the medium are. In solids, the molecules are very close together, so sound moves very fast. In liquids, the molecules have more space around them than in solids, so the sound waves do not move as rapidly. In gases, as in air, the molecules have lots of space around them. Because the molecules are widely spaced, sound waves do not move as fast through gases as through solids or liquids.

The advertisements for a popular science fiction movie stated, "In space, no one can hear

you scream." Is there any basis for this saying? You have seen how the speed of sound varies in different materials and in different conditions. Since sound travels at different rates through different types of solid and liquid materials, it makes sense that sound should travel at different rates through different atmospheres. In this experiment, you will explore how various atmospheres affect how sound waves travel.

What You Need

- A 16-ounce glass jar with a lid
- String
- Tape
- A small bell
- Vinegar
- Baking soda
- Hot water

Sound in a Jar

What You'll Do

#1 Cut a piece of string about 4 inches (10 cm) long.

#2 Tie one end of the string to the bell, and tape the other end of the string to the center of the inside of the jar lid.

#3 Carefully screw the lid on the jar with the bell on the inside. Make sure that the bell does not touch the bottom of the jar. If it does, shorten the length of the string by removing the tape and adjusting the string. Tape the string securely to the lid.

#4 Shake the jar gently and listen to the sound of the bell.

39

#5 Remove the lid of the jar and add two teaspoons of baking soda, 4 tablespoons of vinegar, and 4 tablespoons of water.

#6 After allowing the mixture to fizz for about 30 seconds, replace the lid on the jar.

#7 Shake the jar gently and listen to the sound of the bell.

#8 Remove the lid and rinse out the jar.

#9 Pour hot water into the jar until there is about 1 inch (2.5 cm) of water in it.

Sound in a Jar

#10 Allow the jar to stand undisturbed for about 30 seconds and then replace the lid. Make sure that the bell does not touch the water.

#11 Shake the jar gently and listen to the sound of the bell.

#12 Repeat steps 9 through 11 two more times, leaving the liquid in the jar each time.

Analyzing Your Results

#1 What did you observe about the sound of the bell in this experiment?

#2 How can you explain what you observed?

#3 What are the three different atmospheres you tested in this experiment?

#4 What do your observations reveal about how sound travels in different atmospheres?

#5 In outer space, there is no air at all. What do you think would happen to sound in outer space? Why?

For Further Investigation

Think of some other atmospheres that you could test with this experimental setup. What would the results tell you about how sound travels?

glossary

acoustics   The science of sound.

amplify   To make louder.

chord   A combination of three or more tones played at the same time.

compression   Pressing into a smaller space.

condensation   The area of compression in a medium that a sound wave is moving through.

echo   The repetition of a sound that occurs when sound waves bounce off of a surface.

frequency   The number of vibrations in a sound wave in one second.

hair cells   Tiny cells in the inner ear that respond to sound.

medium   A substance that sound waves travel through. A medium can be a solid, a liquid, or a gas.

molecules   The tiny particles that make up all matter.

pitch   The position of a tone in relation to higher and lower tones.

rarefaction   The area into which a medium expands as a sound wave passes through it.

tone   A sound of a distinct pitch.

wave   A movement in a medium by which energy is transferred from one molecule to another.

resources

These Web sites will help you find out more about sound.

Cool Science for Curious Kids
http://www.hhmi.org/coolscience

Cyberspace Middle School—Science Fair Projects
http://www.scri.fsu.edu/~dennisl/special/sf_projects.html

Exploratorium
http://www.exploratorium.edu

The Franklin Institute
http://sln.fi.edu

Mad Scientist Network
http://www.madsci.org

National Science Foundation's Science in the Home
http://www.her.nsf.gov/ehr/ehr/science_home/html/
    default.htm

Newton Ask a Scientist
http://newton.dep.anl.gov/aasquest.htm

Physics of Sound
http://online.anu.edu.au/ITA/ACAT/drw/PPofM/index.html

The Science Club
http://www.halcyon.com/sciclub

resources

Science Fair Project Ideas
http://othello.mech.nwu.edu/~peshkin/scifair/index.html

Scientific American Explore!
http://www.sciam.com/explorations

Smithsonian Institute
http://www.si.edu

The Soundry
http://hyperion.advanced.org/19537

for further reading

Darling, David. *Sounds Interesting: The Science of Acoustics.* Parsippany, NJ: Silver Burdett Press, 1991.

Gardner, Robert. *Experimenting with Sound.* Danbury, CT: Franklin Watts, 1991.

Grimshaw, Caroline. *Sound.* Chicago: World Book, 1998.

Kaner, Etta. *Sound Science.* Reading, MA: Addison Wesley Longman, 1991.

Kerrod, Robin. *Sounds and Music.* Tarrytown, NY: Marshall Cavendish, 1991.

Morgan, Sally. *Using Sound.* New York: Facts on File, 1994.

Sabbeth, Alex. *Rubber-Band Banjos and a Java-Jive Bass: Projects and Activities in the Science of Music and Sound.* New York: John Wiley & Sons, 1997.

Seller, Mick. *Sound, Noise, and Music.* Danbury, CT: Franklin Watts, 1993.

Ward, Alan. *Sound.* Broomall, PA: Chelsea House Publishers, 1991.

Wood, Robert W. *Sound Fundamentals: Funtastic Science Activities for Kids.* Broomall, PA: Chelsea House Publishers, 1997.

World Book staff. *Sound.* Chicago: World Book, 1997.

index

credits

About the Author

Allan B. Cobb is a freelance science writer living in central Texas. He has written books, radio scripts, articles, and educational materials concerning different aspects of science. When not writing about science, he enjoys traveling, camping, hiking, and exploring caves.

Photo Credits

Cover photos by Scott Bauer. P. 2 © Barrow/International Stock; p. 12 © Index Stock; p. 19 © Custom Medical; p. 25 © Harvey Lloyd/FPG. All other photographs by Scott Bauer.

Design and Layout

Laura Murawski

Consulting Editor

Amy Haugesag

<table>
<tr><td colspan="2">Metric Conversions
To convert measurements in U.S. units into metric units, use the following formulas:</td></tr>
<tr><td>1 inch = 2.54 centimeters (cm)</td><td>1 ounce = 28.35 grams (g)</td></tr>
<tr><td>1 foot = 0.30 meters (m)</td><td>1 gallon = 3.79 liters (l)</td></tr>
<tr><td>1 mile = 1.609 kilometers (km)</td><td>1 pound = 453.59 grams (g)</td></tr>
</table>